Fundraiser Use of LinkedIn

ISBN: 978-1-57440-296-4
Library of Congress Control Number: 2014946881

Table of Contents

THE QUESTIONNAIRE

Introduction

1. Please provide the following contact information:

   A. Name:
   B. Company:
   C. Work Title:
   D. Country:
   E. Email Address:

2. How many full time equivalent fundraisers or advancement professionals does your organization have?

3. Your organization might best be described as:

   A. Library
   B. College
   C. Other
   D. Foundation
   E. Other (please specify)

Types of LinkedIn Accounts Maintained

4. Does your organization have its own organizational LinkedIn site?

   A. Yes
   B. No

5. Does your organization have a basic LinkedIn account or a premium account?

   A. Basic account
   B. Premium account

6. Which phrase best describes how your organization uses LinkedIn?

   A. We have our own institutional site and we use it extensively
   B. We have our own institutional site but we use it somewhat modestly
   C. We don't have an institutional site but use the personal sites of staffers or consultants

7. If your organization has an institutional LinkedIn site in what year was this presence established?

   A. 2008 – 2010
   B. 2011 – 2012
   C. 2013 - 2014

Use of LinkedIn Paid Ads

8. Have you used LinkedIn paid ads?

   A. Yes
   B. No

9. If so how much did your organization spend in the last year on LinkedIn paid ads?

10. Which of the following have you used: text ads? Text and image ads? Video ads?

    A. Text ads
    B. Text and image ads
    C. Video ads

11. Has your organization ever used any of the following LinkedIn services?

    A. LinkedIn Board Member Connect
    B. LinkedIn Non-Profit Solutions

12. If your organization has added any LinkedIn applications to its LinkedIn site please list those that you have added and why.

LinkedIn as a Research and Lead Development Tool

13. Describe how your organization uses LinkedIn as a tool to locate possible donors? What kind of filters do you use in searching? How does the use of LinkedIn compare to the use of other search resources? How much time do you advise others put in to master use of LinkedIn compared to other options?

Pages and Followers

14. How many fundraisers at your organization have personal pages on LinkedIn?

15. How many followers does your organization have on its LinkedIn sites?

16. How often do you send out posts or updates to your followers?

Endorsements

17. How many endorsements does your fundraising office have on LinkedIn?

Participation in LinkedIn Groups

18. Does your organization participate in any LinkedIn Groups?

    A. Yes
    B. No

19. How many?

20. Which ones?

21. How important are LinkedIn Groups to your fundraising efforts firm and how do you use Groups?

22. Does your organization sponsor its own LinkedIn Group?

    A. Yes
    B. No
    C. No, but planning to start one

23. If your organization has its own LinkedIn Group please describe your experience in developing it.

LinkedIn Page Metrics

24. What metrics do you track on your LinkedIn page? Which are the most important ones and why?

25. Rank your presence on LinkedIn as a marketing tool compared to: Facebook, Google+?

    A. Facebook
    B. Google+
    C. Twitter
    D. YouTube

E. LinkedIn

Job Postings on LinkedIn

26. Does your firm post available jobs on LinkedIn?

    A. Yes
    B. No

27. How much did your firm spend over the past year on job posts on LinkedIn?

InMail

28. What is the firm's policy on sending out LinkedIn Invitations?

29. How many InMail messages does the firm send per month?

LinkedIn Content Development

30. Describe the process that your firm uses to develop LinkedIn profiles for your fundrasiers. Do they write and post the profiles themselves? Are they edited by an online marketing specialist to insure proper key word usage and other practices to assure their effectiveness? What practices has your firm developed and what have been the results?

31. Does your organization have a policy of providing content, or content development assistance, to individuals so that they can promote the firm through their personal LinkedIn pages? If so what kind of assistance do you provide?

32. As an educated guess what percentage of your LinkedIn updates from your organization's LinkedIn page include photos, videos or other visual materials?

Parting Advice

33. How would you advise your peers on the most effective ways to use LinkedIn?

SURVEY PARTICIPANTS

Arcadia University
Big Thought
California State University San Marcos
Carolina Christian College
Cathedral Arts Project Inc.
Claremont School of Theology
College of the Atlantic
Drayson Research
EverTrue
Freed-Hardeman University
Home For Our Troops
Hunter College
Idaho State University
Jerold Panas, Linzy & Partners
Kentucky Christian University
Lawrence Technological University
Lebanon Valley College
Midwestern University
Richmond SPCA
Saint Mary's University of Minnesota
St. Olaf College
Stevens Institute of Technology
TATE
The American University of Paris
The Hotchkiss School
The Valley Hospital Foundation
Trinity University
UC Santa Cruz
Union College
University of Arkansas Fort Smith
University of Central Missouri
University of New Hampshire
University of Texas of the Permian Basin
Wentworth Military Academy and Junior College
Wesley College
Whitworth University
World Animal Protection

SUMMARY OF MAIN FINDINGS

Characteristics of the Sample

The mean number of fundraisers employed by the organizations in the sample was 9.83th a median of 5 and a range of 0 to 65. The mean is the average, the total number in the sample divided by the number of survey participants while the median is the "mid-point" in the sample with an equal number of survey participants having more than or less than this number of fundraisers employed. Organizations in the "more than 9" category denoting the number of fundraisers in their organization had a mean of 22.75. Colleges in the sample had a mean of 8.67 fundraisers while other organizations in the sample had a mean of 13.44.

Organizations sampled that had a premium as opposed to a basic LinkedIn account had a mean of 19.5 fundraisers on staff while those with a basic account had a mean of 7.96.

Nearly 74% of the organizations in the sample were colleges and the rest tended to be charities and foundations, often devoted to single causes, such as animal rights.

Nearly 81% of the colleges surveyed had an organizational LinkedIn account while only a little more than 58% of the other non-profits surveyed had an organizational account, as opposed to using a staff members LinkedIn account. Overall 68.42% of organizations surveyed had their own LinkedIn accounts while 31.58% used the personal accounts of staff members.

68.42% of the survey participants had a basic LinkedIn account while 15.79% had a premium account. 30.77% of organizations with more than 9 fundraisers on staff had a premium account. Only 10.71% of colleges surveyed had a premium account.

We asked the survey participants which phrase best described how their organization uses LinkedIn and we gave them three choices: 1) We have our own institutional site and we use it extensively- 2) We have our own institutional site but we use it somewhat modestly- 3) We don't have an institutional site but use the personal sites of staffers or consultants.

Only colleges said that they have their own institutional site and that they use it extensively and 21.43 of colleges gave this answer while no other survey participants gave this answer. Also, more than 57% of colleges said that they have their own site and use it somewhat modestly while only 40% of other non-profits said this. 60% of non-college non-profits use the personal LinkedIn sites of their staffers while less than 18% of college participants did this.

Year LinkedIn Presence Established

Nearly 58% of participants did not answer a question about when their LinkedIn site was established perhaps because they did not know or did not have an organizational site. A plurality that answered the question established their organizational site in 2011 or 2012. Smaller organizations tended to have established their sites most recently. All premium account holders established their sites in 2011 or 2012.

13.16% of organizations sampled have used LinkedIn paid ads. 30% of non-college and 7.14% of colleges in the sample have used LinkedIn paid ads. All users of LinkedIn paid ads had an organizational LinkedIn account, mostly a premium account.

10.53% have used text ads while 7.89% have used text and image ads. Only 2.63% of organizations sampled have used LinkedIn video ads. The video ad user was a college with more than 9 fundraisers.

We asked about use of LinkedIn special services such as Board Member Connect. Only 2.63% had used Board Member Connect, once again a college. 2.63% had used LinkedIn's Non-Profit Solutions, again a college.

Use of LinkedIn in Research

A mean of 7.61 fundraisers at the organizations sampled have personal pages on LinkedIn; the median was 5 and the range 0 to 52.

Number of followers/Endorsements on LinkedIn

The mean number of followers on LinkedIn for the organizations in the sample was 6,654, though the median was only 1684. Colleges had a mean of 6.349 followers while other organizations in the sample had a mean of 8,383. Organizations with their own institutional site had a mean of 7,794 followers with a median of 1,794. None of the organizations in the sample reported endorsements on LinkedIn.

Participation in LinkedIn Groups

26.32% of the organizations sampled participated in a LinkedIn Group. Close to 54% of organizations with more than 9 fundraisers on staff participated in a LinkedIn Group. 32.14% of college fundraisers in the sample participate in LinkedIn Groups while only 10% of other organizations in the sample did so. Only a third of premium account holders participated in LinkedIn Groups. The mean number of LinkedIn Groups participated in was only 1.86 with a median of 1 and a range of 1-5. Colleges tended to participate in alumni-related groups. For the most part fundraisers did not consider LinkedIn Groups to be particularly useful in fundraising but use of it for fundraising purposes appears to be growing as fundraisers see their potential.

More than 34% of the organizations sampled say that they sponsor their own LinkedIn Groups and 5.26% say that they are in the process of developing their own LinkedIn Group.

All those planning to develop a group had fewer than 4 fundraisers on staff and all were colleges.

Percentage of LinkedIn Updates that Include Photos, Videos or Other Visual Materials

An estimated 14.29% of LinkedIn updates made by the survey respondents include photos, videos or other visual materials. The median was 0 and most respondents did not include visual materials in their LinkedIn updates, but the range was 0 to 80% of updates including such materials. Larger organizations were much more likely than smaller ones to include visual materials in their LinkedIn updates; 26.43% of the updates made by organizations with more than 9 fundraisers on staff included visual materials. Colleges, too, were much more likely than non-colleges to include visual materials in their LinkedIn updates; 20% of the updates made by survey respondents from institutions of higher education included visual materials while all non-colleges in the sample did not ever include visual materials in their LinkedIn updates. Organizations that had a premium account were also much more enthusiastic in their use of visual materials in their LinkedIn updates; 37.5% of their updates to LinkedIn included such materials.

LinkedIn Compared to Facebook, Google+, Twitter & YouTube as Marketing Tools

We asked the organizations surveyed to compare LinkedIn as an organizational marketing tool to Facebook, Google+, Twitter & YouTube. We have to say that we were somewhat surprised and disappointed by the results. We asked the survey participants to specifically rank the five sites for their value to them as a marketing and promotional tool. Only 7.89% of the organizations sampled chose LinkedIn as their most important marketing vehicle among these 5 sites, particularly disappointing since the sample base included only companies that made at least some use of LinkedIn, creating a form of selection bias that would tend to inflate LinkedIn's usefulness in a comparative question of this type. In a survey that asked about all five and did not have as a precondition some, even very minimal use of LinkedIn, the results probably would show even fewer companies ranking LinkedIn first. Another 13.16% ranked LinkedIn second, and 18.42% ranked LinkedIn third and a plurality of 28.95% ranked it fourth. 21.05% had LinkedIn ranked fifth, or last, nearly 3 times the number that ranked it first.

Larger organizations were much more likely than smaller ones to rank LinkedIn highly. For example, among organizations with more than 9 full time equivalent fundraisers on staff, 15.38% ranked LinkedIn first, and 23.08% ranked it second with the same percentage ranking it third. Also, as might be expected, all of those ranking LinkedIn first or second had an organizational LinkedIn account, rather than using employee personal accounts.

Nonetheless LinkedIn fared particularly poorly vis a vis Facebook, which was chosen as the most important marketing and promotion vehicle 82.14% of colleges ranked Facebook as their most important fundraising tool, among the five choices presented. Google+ fared much worse than both LinkedIn and Facebook and was the first choice for just 2.63% of survey participants and the second choice for 13.16%. 52.63% ranked it last among their choices.

Twitter was ranked first by only 5.26% of survey respondents but second by 44.74%. of respondents. YouTube was not ranked first by any of the respondents but was ranked second by 13.16% and third by 39.47%.

Posting of Available Jobs on LinkedIn

23.68% of the organizations sampled post available jobs on LinkedIn, including approximately 18% of colleges and 40% of other organizations. Mean spending was $170.

Invitations and InMail

Few organizations sampled had a policy on sending out LinkedIn invitations and most did not appear to use the InMail function of LinkedIn. The mean number of InMail messages sent per month was 0.91 with a median of 0 and a range of 0 to 10. All use was accounted for by organizations with less than 4 fundraisers on staff and all were colleges with a basic LinkedIn account.

Development of LinkedIn Profiles

For the most part LinkedIn profiles are developed individually without centralized direction or requirements. Generally, no content or help is provided.

Percentage of LinkedIn Updates that Include Photos, Videos or Other Visual Materials

An estimated 14.29% of LinkedIn updates made by the survey respondents include photos, videos or other visual materials. The median was 0 and most respondents did not include visual materials in their LinkedIn updates, but the range was 0 to 80% of updates including such materials. Larger organizations were m Much more likely than smaller ones to include visual materials in their LinkedIn updates; 26.43% of the updates made by organizations with more than 9 fundraisers on staff included visual materials. Colleges, too, were much more likely than non-colleges to include visual materials in their LinkedIn updates; 20% of the updates made by survey respondents from institutions of higher education included visual materials while all non-colleges in the sample did not ever include visual materials in their LinkedIn updates. Organizations that had a premium account were also much more enthusiastic in their use of visual materials in their LinkedIn updates; 37.5% of their updates to LinkedIn included such materials.

SECTION A: CHARACTERISTICS OF THE SAMPLE

Table 1.1 How many full time equivalent fundraisers or advancement professionals does your organization have?

	Mean	Median	Minimum	Maximum
Entire sample	9,83	5,00	0,00	65,00

Table 1.2 How many full time equivalent fundraisers or advancement professionals does your organization have? Broken out by Number of FTE Fundraisers

Number of FTE Fundraisers	Mean	Median	Minimum	Maximum
less than 4	1,94	2,00	0,00	4,00
from 4 to 9	5,46	5,00	4,00	9,00
more than 9	22,75	18,50	9,00	65,00

Table 1.3 How many full time equivalent fundraisers or advancement professionals does your organization have? Broken out by Type of Organization

Type of Organization	Mean	Median	Minimum	Maximum
College	8,67	5,00	0,00	40,00
Other	13,44	5,00	0,00	65,00

Table 1.4 How many full time equivalent fundraisers or advancement professionals does your organization have? Broken out by Type of LinkedIn site

Type of LinkedIn site	Mean	Median	Minimum	Maximum
Uses Organizational LinkedIn Account	11,63	5,00	0,00	65,00
Uses Staff Member Personal LinkedIn Accounts	6,08	4,00	0,00	32,00

Table 1.5 How many full time equivalent fundraisers or advancement professionals does your organization have? Broken out by Type of LinkedIn Account

Type of LinkedIn Account	Mean	Median	Minimum	Maximum
Premium account	19,50	22,00	0,00	40,00
Basic account	7,96	5,00	0,00	65,00

Table 2.1 Your organization might best be described as:

	College	Museum	Other
Entire sample	73,68%	2,63%	23,68%

Table 2.2 Your organization might best be described as: Broken out by Number of FTE Fundraisers

Number of FTE Fundraisers	College	Museum	Other
less than 4	69,23%	0,00%	30,77%
from 4 to 9	75,00%	0,00%	25,00%
more than 9	76,92%	7,69%	15,38%

Table 2.3 Your organization might best be described as: Broken out by Type of Organization

Type of Organization	College	Museum	Other
College	100,00%	0,00%	0,00%
Other	0,00%	10,00%	90,00%

Table 2.4 Your organization might best be described as: Broken out by Type of LinkedIn site

Type of LinkedIn site	College	Museum	Other
Uses Organizational LinkedIn Account	80,77%	3,85%	15,38%
Uses Staff Member Personal LinkedIn Accounts	58,33%	0,00%	41,67%

Table 2.5 Your organization might best be described as: Broken out by Type of LinkedIn Account

Type of LinkedIn Account	College	Museum	Other
Premium account	50,00%	0,00%	50,00%
Basic account	78,13%	3,13%	18,75%

SECTION B: TYPES OF LINKEDIN ACCOUNTS MAINTAINED

Table 3.1 Does your organization have its own organizational LinkedIn site?

	No Answer	Yes	No
Entire sample	0,00%	68,42%	31,58%

Table 3.2 Does your organization have its own organizational LinkedIn site? Broken out by Number of FTE Fundraisers

Number of FTE Fundraisers	Yes	No
less than 4	53,85%	46,15%
from 4 to 9	66,67%	33,33%
more than 9	84,62%	15,38%

Table 3.3 Does your organization have its own organizational LinkedIn site? Broken out by Type of Organization

Type of Organization	Yes	No
College	75,00%	25,00%
Other	50,00%	50,00%

Table 3.4 Does your organization have its own organizational LinkedIn site? Broken out by Type of LinkedIn site

Type of LinkedIn site	Yes	No
Uses Organizational LinkedIn Account	100,00%	0,00%
Uses Staff Member Personal LinkedIn Accounts	0,00%	100,00%

Table 3.5 Does your organization have its own organizational LinkedIn site? Broken out by Type of LinkedIn Account

Type of LinkedIn Account	Yes	No
Premium account	66,67%	33,33%
Basic account	68,75%	31,25%

Table 4.1 Does your organization have a basic LinkedIn account or a premium account?

	Basic account	Premium account	No answer
Entire sample	68,42%	15,79%	15,79%

Table 4.2 Does your organization have a basic LinkedIn account or a premium account? Broken out by Number of FTE Fundraisers

Number of FTE Fundraisers	Basic account	Premium account	No answer
less than 4	53,85%	15,38%	30,77%
from 4 to 9	83,33%	0,00%	16,67%
more than 9	69,23%	30,77%	0,00%

Table 4.3 Does your organization have a basic LinkedIn account or a premium account? Broken out by Type of Organization

Type of Organization	Basic account	Premium account	No answer
College	67,86%	10,71%	21,43%
Other	70,00%	30,00%	0,00%

Table 4.4 Does your organization have a basic LinkedIn account or a premium account? Broken out by Type of LinkedIn site

Type of LinkedIn site	Basic account	Premium account	No answer
Uses Organizational LinkedIn Account	84,62%	15,38%	0,00%
Uses Staff Member Personal LinkedIn Accounts	33,33%	16,67%	50,00%

Table 4.5 Does your organization have a basic LinkedIn account or a premium account? Broken out by Type of LinkedIn Account

Type of LinkedIn Account	Basic account	Premium account	No answer
Premium account	0,00%	100,00%	0,00%
Basic account	81,25%	0,00%	18,75%

Table 5.1 Which phrase best describes how your organization uses LinkedIn?

	No Answer	We have our own institutional site and we use it extensively	We have our own institutional site but we use it somewhat modestly	We don't have an institutional site but use the personal sites of staffers or consultants
Entire sample	2,63%	15,79%	52,63%	28,95%

Table 5.2 Which phrase best describes how your organization uses LinkedIn? Broken out by Number of FTE Fundraisers

Number of FTE Fundraisers	No Answer	We have our own institutional site and we use it extensively	We have our own institutional site but we use it somewhat modestly	We don't have an institutional site but use the personal sites of staffers or consultants
less than 4	7,69%	15,38%	46,15%	30,77%
from 4 to 9	0,00%	8,33%	58,33%	33,33%
more than 9	0,00%	23,08%	53,85%	23,08%

Table 5.3 Which phrase best describes how your organization uses LinkedIn? Broken out by Type of Organization

Type of Organization	No Answer	We have our own institutional site and we use it extensively	We have our own institutional site but we use it somewhat modestly	We don't have an institutional site but use the personal sites of staffers or consultants
College	3,57%	21,43%	57,14%	17,86%
Other	0,00%	0,00%	40,00%	60,00%

Table 5.4 Which phrase best describes how your organization uses LinkedIn? Broken out by Type of LinkedIn site

Type of LinkedIn site	No Answer	We have our own institutional site and we use it extensively	We have our own institutional site but we use it somewhat modestly	We don't have an institutional site but use the personal sites of staffers or consultants
Uses Organizational LinkedIn Account	0,00%	19,23%	76,92%	3,85%
Uses Staff Member Personal LinkedIn Accounts	8,33%	8,33%	0,00%	83,33%

Table 5.5 Which phrase best describes how your organization uses LinkedIn? Broken out by Type of LinkedIn Account

Type of LinkedIn Account	No Answer	We have our own institutional site and we use it extensively	We have our own institutional site but we use it somewhat modestly	We don't have an institutional site but use the personal sites of staffers or consultants
Premium account	0,00%	33,33%	33,33%	33,33%
Basic account	3,13%	12,50%	56,25%	28,13%

Table 6.1 If your organization has an institutional LinkedIn site in what year was this presence established?

	No Answer	2008 - 2010	2011 - 2012	2013 - 2014
Entire sample	57,89%	13,16%	18,42%	10,53%

Table 6.2 If your organization has an institutional LinkedIn site in what year was this presence established? Broken out by Number of FTE Fundraisers

Number of FTE Fundraisers	No Answer	2008 - 2010	2011 - 2012	2013 - 2014
less than 4	61,54%	7,69%	7,69%	23,08%
from 4 to 9	66,67%	16,67%	8,33%	8,33%
more than 9	46,15%	15,38%	38,46%	0,00%

Table 6.3 If your organization has an institutional LinkedIn site in what year was this presence established? Broken out by Type of Organization

Type of Organization	No Answer	2008 - 2010	2011 - 2012	2013 - 2014
College	53,57%	14,29%	17,86%	14,29%
Other	70,00%	10,00%	20,00%	0,00%

Table 6.4 If your organization has an institutional LinkedIn site in what year was this presence established? Broken out by Type of LinkedIn site

Type of LinkedIn site	No Answer	2008 - 2010	2011 - 2012	2013 - 2014
Uses Organizational LinkedIn Account	38,46%	19,23%	26,92%	15,38%

Table 6.5 If your organization has an institutional LinkedIn site in what year was this presence established? Broken out by Type of LinkedIn Account

Type of LinkedIn Account	No Answer	2008 - 2010	2011 - 2012	2013 - 2014
Premium account	50,00%	0,00%	50,00%	0,00%
Basic account	59,38%	15,63%	12,50%	12,50%

SECTION C: USE OF LINKEDIN PAID ADS

Table 7.1 Have you used LinkedIn paid ads?

	No Answer	Yes	No
Entire sample	2,63%	13,16%	84,21%

Table 7.2 Have you used LinkedIn paid ads? Broken out by Number of FTE Fundraisers

Number of FTE Fundraisers	No Answer	Yes	No
less than 4	7,69%	7,69%	84,62%
from 4 to 9	0,00%	16,67%	83,33%
more than 9	0,00%	15,38%	84,62%

Table 7.3 Have you used LinkedIn paid ads? Broken out by Type of Organization

Type of Organization	No Answer	Yes	No
College	3,57%	7,14%	89,29%
Other	0,00%	30,00%	70,00%

Table 7.4 Have you used LinkedIn paid ads? Broken out by Type of LinkedIn site

Type of LinkedIn site	No Answer	Yes	No
Uses Organizational LinkedIn Account	0,00%	19,23%	80,77%
Uses Staff Member Personal LinkedIn Accounts	8,33%	0,00%	91,67%

Table 7.5 Have you used LinkedIn paid ads? Broken out by Type of LinkedIn Account

Type of LinkedIn Account	No Answer	Yes	No
Premium account	0,00%	33,33%	66,67%
Basic account	3,13%	9,38%	87,50%

Table 8.1 If so how much did your organization spend ($) in the last year on LinkedIn paid ads?

	Mean	Median	Minimum	Maximum
Entire sample	2000,00	500,00	0,00	7000,00

Table 8.2 If so how much did your organization spend ($) in the last year on LinkedIn paid ads? Broken out by Number of FTE Fundraisers

Number of FTE Fundraisers	Mean	Median	Minimum	Maximum
less than 4	7000,00	7000,00	7000,00	7000,00
from 4 to 9	500,00	500,00	0,00	1000,00
more than 9	0,00	0,00	0,00	0,00

Table 8.3 If so how much did your organization spend ($) in the last year on LinkedIn paid ads? Broken out by Type of Organization

Type of Organization	Mean	Median	Minimum	Maximum
College	0,00	0,00	0,00	0,00
Other	4000,00	4000,00	1000,00	7000,00

Table 8.4 If so how much did your organization spend ($) in the last year on LinkedIn paid ads? Broken out by Type of LinkedIn site

Type of LinkedIn site	Mean	Median	Minimum	Maximum
Uses Organizational LinkedIn Account	2000,00	500,00	0,00	7000,00

Table 8.5 If so how much did your organization spend ($) in the last year on LinkedIn paid ads? Broken out by Type of LinkedIn Account

Type of LinkedIn Account	Mean	Median	Minimum	Maximum
Premium account	7000,00	7000,00	7000,00	7000,00
Basic account	333,33	0,00	0,00	1000,00

SECTION D: TYPES OF LINKEDIN ADS USED

Table 9 Which of the following have you used: text ads? Text and image ads? Video ads?

Table 9.1.1 Has your organization ever used LinkedIn Text ads?

	No Answer	Yes	No
Entire sample	0,00%	10,53%	89,47%

Table 9.1.2 Has your organization ever used LinkedIn Text ads? Broken out by Number of FTE Fundraisers

Number of FTE Fundraisers	Yes	No
less than 4	7,69%	92,31%
from 4 to 9	8,33%	91,67%
more than 9	15,38%	84,62%

Table 9.1.3 Has your organization ever used LinkedIn Text ads? Broken out by Type of Organization

Type of Organization	Yes	No
College	3,57%	96,43%
Other	30,00%	70,00%

Table 9.1.4 Has your organization ever used LinkedIn Text ads? Broken out by Type of LinkedIn site

Type of LinkedIn site	Yes	No
Uses Organizational LinkedIn Account	15,38%	84,62%
Uses Staff Member Personal LinkedIn Accounts	0,00%	100,00%

Table 9.1.5 Has your organization ever used LinkedIn Text ads? Broken out by Type of LinkedIn Account

Type of LinkedIn Account	Yes	No
Premium account	33,33%	66,67%
Basic account	6,25%	93,75%

Table 9.2.1 Has your organization ever used LinkedIn Text and image ads?

	No Answer	Yes	No
Entire sample	0,00%	7,89%	92,11%

Table 9.2. Has your organization ever used LinkedIn Text and image ads? Broken out by Number of FTE Fundraisers

Number of FTE Fundraisers	Yes	No
less than 4	7,69%	92,31%
from 4 to 9	8,33%	91,67%
more than 9	7,69%	92,31%

Table 9.2.3 Has your organization ever used LinkedIn Text and image ads? Broken out by Type of Organization

Type of Organization	Yes	No
College	7,14%	92,86%
Other	10,00%	90,00%

Table 9.2.4 Has your organization ever used LinkedIn Text and image ads? Broken out by Type of LinkedIn site

Type of LinkedIn site	Yes	No
Uses Organizational LinkedIn Account	11,54%	88,46%
Uses Staff Member Personal LinkedIn Accounts	0,00%	100,00%

Table 9.2.5 Has your organization ever used LinkedIn Text and image ads? Broken out by Type of LinkedIn Account

Type of LinkedIn Account	Yes	No
Premium account	33,33%	66,67%
Basic account	3,13%	96,88%

Table 9.3.1 Has your organization ever used LinkedIn Video ads?

	No Answer	Yes	No
Entire sample	0,00%	2,63%	97,37%

Table 9.3.2 Has your organization ever used LinkedIn Video ads? Broken out by Number of FTE Fundraisers

Number of FTE Fundraisers	Yes	No
less than 4	0,00%	100,00%
from 4 to 9	0,00%	100,00%
more than 9	7,69%	92,31%

Table 9.3.3 Has your organization ever used LinkedIn Video ads? Broken out by Type of Organization

Type of Organization	Yes	No
College	3,57%	96,43%
Other	0,00%	100,00%

Table 9.3.4 Has your organization ever used LinkedIn Video ads? Broken out by Type of LinkedIn site

Type of LinkedIn site	Yes	No
Uses Organizational LinkedIn Account	3,85%	96,15%
Uses Staff Member Personal LinkedIn Accounts	0,00%	100,00%

Table 9.3.5 Has your organization ever used LinkedIn Video ads? Broken out by Type of LinkedIn Account

Type of LinkedIn Account	Yes	No
Premium account	16,67%	83,33%
Basic account	0,00%	100,00%

SECTION E: TYPES OF LINKEDIN SERVICES USED

Table 10 Has your organization ever used any of the following LinkedIn services?

Table 10.1.1 Has your organization ever used LinkedIn Board Member Connect?

	No Answer	Yes	No
Entire sample	0,00%	2,63%	97,37%

Table 10.1.2 Has your organization ever used LinkedIn Board Member Connect?Broken out by Number of FTE Fundraisers

Number of FTE Fundraisers	Yes	No
less than 4	0,00%	100,00%
from 4 to 9	8,33%	91,67%
more than 9	0,00%	100,00%

Table 10.1.3 Has your organization ever used LinkedIn Board Member Connect? Broken out by Type of Organization

Type of Organization	Yes	No
College	3,57%	96,43%
Other	0,00%	100,00%

Table 10.1.4 Has your organization ever used LinkedIn Board Member Connect? Broken out by Type of LinkedIn site

Type of LinkedIn site	Yes	No
Uses Organizational LinkedIn Account	3,85%	96,15%
Uses Staff Member Personal LinkedIn Accounts	0,00%	100,00%

Table 10.1.5 Has your organization ever used LinkedIn Board Member Connect? Broken out by Type of LinkedIn Account

Type of LinkedIn Account	Yes	No
Premium account	0,00%	100,00%
Basic account	3,13%	96,88%

Table 10.2.1 Has your organization ever used LinkedIn Non-Profit Solutions?

	No Answer	Yes	No
Entire sample	0,00%	2,63%	97,37%

Table 10.2.2 Has your organization ever used LinkedIn Non-Profit Solutions? Broken out by Number of FTE Fundraisers

Number of FTE Fundraisers	Yes	No
less than 4	0,00%	100,00%
from 4 to 9	8,33%	91,67%
more than 9	0,00%	100,00%

Table 10.2.3 Has your organization ever used LinkedIn Non-Profit Solutions? Broken out by Type of Organization

Type of Organization	Yes	No
College	3,57%	96,43%
Other	0,00%	100,00%

Table 10.2.4 Has your organization ever used LinkedIn Non-Profit Solutions? Broken out by Type of LinkedIn site

Type of LinkedIn site	Yes	No
Uses Organizational LinkedIn Account	3,85%	96,15%
Uses Staff Member Personal LinkedIn Accounts	0,00%	100,00%

Table 10.2.5 Has your organization ever used LinkedIn Non-Profit Solutions? Broken out by Type of LinkedIn Account

Type of LinkedIn Account	Yes	No
Premium account	0,00%	100,00%
Basic account	3,13%	96,88%

Describe how your organization uses LinkedIn as a tool to locate possible donors? What kind of filters do you use in searching? How does the use of LinkedIn compare to the use of other search resources? How much time do you advise others put in to master use of LinkedIn compared to other options?

1) We don't and we need to use it more.
2) I have not used LinkedIn for fundraising.
3) Alumni that work for companies. To contact our alumni. Filter on name, company, title, region, industry. LinkedIn is much more up to date with employment info.
4) We don't use it to identify potential donors, but we do use to to garner information about prospects identified through other means.
5) We have two groups on LinkedIn -- I search for prospects regularly in those two groups.
6) I use it to connect employment history, affiliated organizations, educational connections/degrees, interests, hobbies, undergraduate activities.
7) We don't use it to locate donors. We only use it to collect data
8) We use it only to double check information on prospects identified via other means (i.e. if someone has a common name and is a 3rd connection to the frontline fundraiser, it's likely that we have correctly identified the prospect and their job title).
9) Only use location and school search functions
10) We have been using LinkedIn primarily as a tool to connect with Alumni and former students; it's a preliminary step to having them become donors.
11) Sorting by keyword filters and/or geographic location primarily. LinkedIn appears to be much more accurate and current than anything else. I tell others that LinkedIn is well worth looking into as a research tool.
12) We use LinkedIn but don't show our visibility
13) I teach on this subject extensively. It is a good tool for prospecting but a better tool for research. Filters depend entirely on the engagement/project. It is difficult to compare LI to other research tools except to predecessors in biographical data--which it greatly outshines in every respect. It is easy to master and use LI effectively--the greatest investment of time is in maintaining and nurturing the relationships and toolset.
14) We use it individually, our company page is more or less just something that is used to identify our alumni and friends that have an association with us.
15) We use the University page "where do they work?" feature and search on title and company.
16) We use to update business information for our alumni.
17) We use LinkedIn for alumni searches and benefactor searches. We invite anyone we see with a LinkedIn profile and Saint Mary's degree to join the Saint Mary's page. I use the advanced search most often - searching on titles and/or city/state.
18) We currently use LinkedIn as a way to connect with alumni/ae. We don't use it for fundraising at this time.
19) we don't

20) We haven't yet
21) We don't use it to locate possible donors. We use our alumni database.
22) We have really only used LinkedIn to look for current job information for alumni...basically data mining.
23) We don't use LI to locate donors.
24) We have utilized it as a preliminary screening tool in the prospect identification phase.
25) Right now the site is used more to market to prospective students rather than donors.
26) We don't really use LinkedIn, however, if I run across WMA alumni, I will connect with them.
27) We have not harnessed the opportunity of LinkedIn as the Advancement office is going through radical operational changes with new business model and protocols being written to address 21st century fundraising.
28) LinkedIn is occasionally used in researching prospects once we've identified their name.
29) We are just starting to explore how LinkedIn can benefit our alumni outreach and fundraising goals.
30) We haven't as of yet.
31) We are just beginning to look into the use of LinkedIn as a prospect research tool.
32) We use it primarily as a prospect research tool for titles and names, and occasionally to make contact.
33) We have failed to do this.

SECTION F: LINKED IN PAGES, FOLLOWERS & ENDORSEMENTS

Table 12.1 How many fundraisers at your organization have personal pages on LinkedIn?

	Mean	Median	Minimum	Maximum
Entire sample	7,61	5,00	0,00	52,00

Table 12.2 How many fundraisers at your organization have personal pages on LinkedIn? Broken out by Number of FTE Fundraisers

Number of FTE Fundraisers	Mean	Median	Minimum	Maximum
less than 4	1,83	2,00	0,00	4,00
from 4 to 9	4,54	5,00	2,00	7,00
more than 9	15,50	10,50	6,00	52,00

Table 12.3 How many fundraisers at your organization have personal pages on LinkedIn? Broken out by Type of Organization

Type of Organization	Mean	Median	Minimum	Maximum
College	6,88	5,00	1,00	25,00
Other	10,00	4,50	0,00	52,00

Table 12.4 How many fundraisers at your organization have personal pages on LinkedIn? Broken out by Type of LinkedIn site

Type of LinkedIn site	Mean	Median	Minimum	Maximum
Uses Organizational LinkedIn Account	9,19	5,00	0,00	52,00
Uses Staff Member Personal LinkedIn Accounts	3,22	3,00	1,00	6,00

Table 12.5 How many fundraisers at your organization have personal pages on LinkedIn? Broken out by Type of LinkedIn Account

Type of LinkedIn Account	Mean	Median	Minimum	Maximum
Premium account	16,00	19,50	0,00	25,00
Basic account	6,49	5,00	1,00	52,00

Table 13.1 How many followers does your organization have on its LinkedIn sites?

	Mean	Median	Minimum	Maximum
Entire sample	6654,20	1684,50	0,00	56170,00

Table 13.2 How many followers does your organization have on its LinkedIn sites? Broken out by Number of FTE Fundraisers

Number of FTE Fundraisers	Mean	Median	Minimum	Maximum
less than 4	2056,57	950,00	400,00	8924,00
from 4 to 9	1839,00	1368,00	0,00	6138,00
more than 9	15379,14	6319,00	1788,00	56170,00

Table 13.3 How many followers does your organization have on its LinkedIn sites? Broken out by Type of Organization

Type of Organization	Mean	Median	Minimum	Maximum
College	6349,18	1788,00	360,00	56170,00
Other	8382,67	500,00	0,00	24648,00

Table 13.4 How many followers does your organization have on its LinkedIn sites? Broken out by Type of LinkedIn site

Type of LinkedIn site	Mean	Median	Minimum	Maximum
Uses Organizational LinkedIn Account	7371,33	1794,00	360,00	56170,00
Uses Staff Member Personal LinkedIn Accounts	200,00	200,00	0,00	400,00

Table 13.5 How many followers does your organization have on its LinkedIn sites? Broken out by Type of LinkedIn Account

Type of LinkedIn Account	Mean	Median	Minimum	Maximum
Premium account	5166,67	4000,00	500,00	11000,00
Basic account	6916,71	1581,00	0,00	56170,00

How often do you send out posts or updates to your followers?

1) Not enough
2) 1x month
3) Seldom
4) Unknown
5) Don't know
6) hardly ever
7) never
8) N/A
9) once or twice per quarter
10) I don't
11) Regularly
12) 2 - 5 times per week (personally)
13) Seldom
14) Daily
15) don't know
16) Not often enough
17) Seldom
18) No
19) Once every couple of weeks
20) Weekly
21) Monthly
22) Weekly
23) Not very often.
24) About 3 times per month, pending on group member discussion rates
25) Not used at the present but will be sending messages in the next fiscal year.
26) not very often
27) Monthly
28) n/a
29) Rarely.

Table 14.1 How many endorsements does your fundraising office have on LinkedIn?

	Mean	Median	Minimum	Maximum
Entire sample	0,00	0,00	0,00	0,00

SECTION F: USE OF LINKEDIN GROUPS

Table 15.1 Does your organization participate in any LinkedIn Groups?

	No Answer	Yes	No
Entire sample	7,89%	26,32%	65,79%

Table 15.2 Does your organization participate in any LinkedIn Groups? Broken out by Number of FTE Fundraisers

Number of FTE Fundraisers	No Answer	Yes	No
less than 4	0,00%	23,08%	76,92%
from 4 to 9	16,67%	0,00%	83,33%
more than 9	7,69%	53,85%	38,46%

Table 15.3 Does your organization participate in any LinkedIn Groups? Broken out by Type of Organization

Type of Organization	No Answer	Yes	No
College	7,14%	32,14%	60,71%
Other	10,00%	10,00%	80,00%

Table 15.4 Does your organization participate in any LinkedIn Groups? Broken out by Type of LinkedIn site

Type of LinkedIn site	No Answer	Yes	No
Uses Organizational LinkedIn Account	7,69%	30,77%	61,54%
Uses Staff Member Personal LinkedIn Accounts	8,33%	16,67%	75,00%

Table 15.5 Does your organization participate in any LinkedIn Groups? Broken out by Type of LinkedIn Account

Type of LinkedIn Account	No Answer	Yes	No
Premium account	16,67%	33,33%	50,00%
Basic account	6,25%	25,00%	68,75%

Table 16.1 In how many LinkedIn Groups does your organization participate?

	Mean	Median	Minimum	Maximum
Entire sample	1,86	1,00	0,00	5,00

Table 16.2 In how many LinkedIn Groups does your organization participate? Broken out by Number of FTE Fundraisers

Number of FTE Fundraisers	Mean	Median	Minimum	Maximum
less than 4	2,25	2,00	0,00	5,00
more than 9	1,33	1,00	0,00	3,00

Table 16.3 In how many LinkedIn Groups does your organization participate? Broken out by Type of Organization

Type of Organization	Mean	Median	Minimum	Maximum
College	2,17	2,00	0,00	5,00
Other	0,00	0,00	0,00	0,00

Table 16.4 In how many LinkedIn Groups does your organization participate? Broken out by Type of LinkedIn site

Type of LinkedIn site	Mean	Median	Minimum	Maximum
Uses Organizational LinkedIn Account	1,25	1,00	0,00	3,00
Uses Staff Member Personal LinkedIn Accounts	2,67	3,00	0,00	5,00

Table 16.5 In how many LinkedIn Groups does your organization participate? Broken out by Type of LinkedIn Account

Type of LinkedIn Account	Mean	Median	Minimum	Maximum
Premium account	1,00	1,00	1,00	1,00
Basic account	2,00	2,00	0,00	5,00

Which ones?

1) Fundraising Alumni
2) alumni-centered groups initiated by alumni and usually geographically focused
3) ?
4) See above
5) Alumni/ae group
6) NCS4 Southern Miss. 1st NCS4 at National Center for Spectator Sports Safety and Security
7) Not sure
8) Arcadia University Alumni, a Young Alumni group and an Arcadia University group

How important are LinkedIn Groups to your fundraising efforts firm and how do you use Groups?

1) Yes, I use the groups aspect and the news feed links.
2) We don't
3) Very important I prospect in the groups
4) We are just beginning to use LinkedIn as an alumni-relations and fundraising tool, so as yet, LinkedIn Groups are not a strong component of our efforts.
5) Moderate
6) They are very important for engagement, but we have just started to make the occasional fundraising post.
7) We haven't done a lot of fundraising on LinkedIn. Our Alumni Association is the largest group we have at this time.
8) not really
9) somewhat
10) not at all important
11) Not really at all
12) Not very
13) I use mine for my own professional development and to get ideas from peers.
14) Not important at all yet.
15) Not at all.

Table 17.1 Does your organization sponsor its own LinkedIn Group?

	No Answer	Yes	No	No, but planning to start one
Entire sample	10,53%	34,21%	50,00%	5,26%

Table 17.2 Does your organization sponsor its own LinkedIn Group? Broken out by Number of FTE Fundraisers

Number of FTE Fundraisers	No Answer	Yes	No	No, but planning to start one
less than 4	0,00%	15,38%	69,23%	15,38%
from 4 to 9	25,00%	33,33%	41,67%	0,00%
more than 9	7,69%	53,85%	38,46%	0,00%

Table 17.3 Does your organization sponsor its own LinkedIn Group? Broken out by Type of Organization

Type of Organization	No Answer	Yes	No	No, but planning to start one
College	10,71%	46,43%	35,71%	7,14%
Other	10,00%	0,00%	90,00%	0,00%

Table 17.4 Does your organization sponsor its own LinkedIn Group? Broken out by Type of LinkedIn site

Type of LinkedIn site	No Answer	Yes	No	No, but planning to start one
Uses Organizational LinkedIn Account	7,69%	42,31%	46,15%	3,85%
Uses Staff Member Personal LinkedIn Accounts	16,67%	16,67%	58,33%	8,33%

Table 17.5 Does your organization sponsor its own LinkedIn Group? Broken out by Type of LinkedIn Account

Type of LinkedIn Account	No Answer	Yes	No	No, but planning to start one
Premium account	16,67%	50,00%	33,33%	0,00%
Basic account	9,38%	31,25%	53,13%	6,25%

If your organization has its own LinkedIn Group please describe your experience in developing it.

1) I did not develop.
2) for various constituencies at the university
3) An alumnus developed it for us.
4) We have a manager on staff but it basically develops itself, we do not have to market it.
5) We created an Alumni/ae Group within our school's LinkedIn page. It was pretty easy to develop.
6) Wasn't involved
7) Still in the development stage.
8) Other than creating it and occasionally adding to the content, nothing

What metrics do you track on your LinkedIn page? Which are the most important ones and why?

1) We don't.
2) I have not tracked.
3) Unknown
4) N/A
5) Number of members
6) N/A
7) Numbers of alumni listed and numbers of alumni following our page.
8) None
9) We don't track anything.
10) Since we are pretty new to this, the most important metric is number of followers
11) None
12) Number involved
13) Followers, # of alumni
14) None
15) Too new, not tracking activity at this time.
16) none yet

SECTION G: LINKED IN AS A MARKETING TOOL COMPARED TO FACEBOOK, GOOGLE+, TWITTER, & YOUTUBE

Table 18 Rank your presence on LinkedIn as a marketing tool compared to: Facebook, Google+, Twitter, YouTube

Table 18.1.1 Rank your presence on LinkedIn as a marketing tool compared to: Facebook, Google+, Twitter, YouTube

	No Answer	Ranked First	Ranked Second	Ranked Third	Ranked Fourth	Ranked Fifth
Entire sample	10,53%	7,89%	13,16%	18,42%	28,95%	21,05%

Table 18.1.2 Rank your presence on LinkedIn as a marketing tool compared to: Facebook, Google+, Twitter, YouTube Broken out by Number of FTE Fundraisers

Number of FTE Fundraisers	No Answer	Ranked First	Ranked Second	Ranked Third	Ranked Fourth	Ranked Fifth
less than 4	15,38%	7,69%	7,69%	15,38%	23,08%	30,77%
from 4 to 9	8,33%	0,00%	8,33%	16,67%	50,00%	16,67%
more than 9	7,69%	15,38%	23,08%	23,08%	15,38%	15,38%

Table 18.1.3 Rank your presence on LinkedIn as a marketing tool compared to: Facebook, Google+, Twitter, YouTube Broken out by Type of Organization

Type of Organization	No Answer	Ranked First	Ranked Second	Ranked Third	Ranked Fourth	Ranked Fifth
College	3,57%	7,14%	17,86%	25,00%	25,00%	21,43%
Other	30,00%	10,00%	0,00%	0,00%	40,00%	20,00%

Table 18.1.4 Rank your presence on LinkedIn as a marketing tool compared to: Facebook, Google+, Twitter, YouTube Broken out by Type of LinkedIn site

Type of LinkedIn site	No Answer	Ranked First	Ranked Second	Ranked Third	Ranked Fourth	Ranked Fifth
Uses Organizational LinkedIn Account	3,85%	11,54%	19,23%	23,08%	26,92%	15,38%
Uses Staff Member Personal LinkedIn Accounts	25,00%	0,00%	0,00%	8,33%	33,33%	33,33%

Table 18.1.5 Rank your presence on LinkedIn as a marketing tool compared to: Facebook, Google+, Twitter, YouTube Broken out by Type of LinkedIn Account

Type of LinkedIn Account	No Answer	Ranked First	Ranked Second	Ranked Third	Ranked Fourth	Ranked Fifth
Premium account	33,33%	16,67%	33,33%	16,67%	0,00%	0,00%
Basic account	6,25%	6,25%	9,38%	18,75%	34,38%	25,00%

Table 18.2.1 Rank your presence on Facebook as a marketing tool compared to: Google+, Twitter, YouTube, LinkedIn

	No Answer	Ranked First	Ranked Second	Ranked Third	Ranked Fourth	Ranked Fifth
Entire sample	13,16%	73,68%	5,26%	7,89%	0,00%	0,00%

Table 18.2.2 Rank your presence on Facebook as a marketing tool compared to: Google+, Twitter, YouTube, LinkedIn. Broken out by Number of FTE Fundraisers

Number of FTE Fundraisers	No Answer	Ranked First	Ranked Second	Ranked Third	Ranked Fourth	Ranked Fifth
less than 4	15,38%	69,23%	0,00%	15,38%	0,00%	0,00%
from 4 to 9	16,67%	83,33%	0,00%	0,00%	0,00%	0,00%
more than 9	7,69%	69,23%	15,38%	7,69%	0,00%	0,00%

Table 18.2.3 Rank your presence on Facebook as a marketing tool compared to: Google+, Twitter, YouTube, LinkedIn. Broken out by Type of Organization

Type of Organization	No Answer	Ranked First	Ranked Second	Ranked Third	Ranked Fourth	Ranked Fifth
College	7,14%	82,14%	3,57%	7,14%	0,00%	0,00%
Other	30,00%	50,00%	10,00%	10,00%	0,00%	0,00%

Table 18.2.4 Rank your presence on Facebook as a marketing tool compared to: Google+, Twitter, YouTube, LinkedIn. Broken out by Type of LinkedIn site

Type of LinkedIn site	No Answer	Ranked First	Ranked Second	Ranked Third	Ranked Fourth	Ranked Fifth
Uses Organizational LinkedIn Account	7,69%	76,92%	7,69%	7,69%	0,00%	0,00%
Uses Staff Member Personal LinkedIn Accounts	25,00%	66,67%	0,00%	8,33%	0,00%	0,00%

Table 18.2.5 Rank your presence on Facebook as a marketing tool compared to: Google+, Twitter, YouTube, LinkedIn. Broken out by Type of LinkedIn Account

Type of LinkedIn Account	No Answer	Ranked First	Ranked Second	Ranked Third	Ranked Fourth	Ranked Fifth
Premium account	33,33%	50,00%	0,00%	16,67%	0,00%	0,00%
Basic account	9,38%	78,13%	6,25%	6,25%	0,00%	0,00%

Table 18.3.1 Rank your presence on Google+ as a marketing tool compared to Facebook, Twitter, YouTube, LinkedIn

	No Answer	Ranked First	Ranked Second	Ranked Third	Ranked Fourth	Ranked Fifth
Entire sample	10,53%	2,63%	13,16%	5,26%	15,79%	52,63%

Table 18.3.2 Rank your presence on Google+ as a marketing tool compared to Facebook, Twitter, YouTube, LinkedIn. Broken out by Number of FTE Fundraisers

Number of FTE Fundraisers	No Answer	Ranked First	Ranked Second	Ranked Third	Ranked Fourth	Ranked Fifth
less than 4	15,38%	7,69%	7,69%	0,00%	23,08%	46,15%
from 4 to 9	8,33%	0,00%	16,67%	0,00%	16,67%	58,33%
more than 9	7,69%	0,00%	15,38%	15,38%	7,69%	53,85%

Table 1.2.3 Rank your presence on Google+ as a marketing tool compared to Facebook, Twitter, YouTube, LinkedIn. Broken out by Type of Organization

Type of Organization	No Answer	Ranked First	Ranked Second	Ranked Third	Ranked Fourth	Ranked Fifth
College	3,57%	3,57%	17,86%	3,57%	14,29%	57,14%
Other	30,00%	0,00%	0,00%	10,00%	20,00%	40,00%

Table 18.3.4 Rank your presence on Google+ as a marketing tool compared to Facebook, Twitter, YouTube, LinkedIn. Broken out by Type of LinkedIn site

Type of LinkedIn site	No Answer	Ranked First	Ranked Second	Ranked Third	Ranked Fourth	Ranked Fifth
Uses Organizational LinkedIn Account	3,85%	0,00%	15,38%	7,69%	15,38%	57,69%
Uses Staff Member Personal LinkedIn Accounts	25,00%	8,33%	8,33%	0,00%	16,67%	41,67%

Table 18.3.5 Rank your presence on Google+ as a marketing tool compared to Facebook, Twitter, YouTube, LinkedIn. Broken out by Type of LinkedIn Account

Type of LinkedIn Account	No Answer	Ranked First	Ranked Second	Ranked Third	Ranked Fourth	Ranked Fifth
Premium account	33,33%	0,00%	0,00%	16,67%	16,67%	33,33%
Basic account	6,25%	3,13%	15,63%	3,13%	15,63%	56,25%

Table 18.4.1 Rank your presence on Twitter as a marketing tool compared to Facebook, Google+, YouTube, LinkedIn

	No Answer	Ranked First	Ranked Second	Ranked Third	Ranked Fourth	Ranked Fifth
Entire sample	10,53%	5,26%	44,74%	18,42%	18,42%	2,63%

Table 18.4.2 Rank your presence on Twitter as a marketing tool compared to Facebook, Google+, YouTube, LinkedIn. Broken out by Number of FTE Fundraisers

Number of FTE Fundraisers	No Answer	Ranked First	Ranked Second	Ranked Third	Ranked Fourth	Ranked Fifth
less than 4	15,38%	0,00%	53,85%	15,38%	15,38%	0,00%
from 4 to 9	8,33%	8,33%	50,00%	25,00%	0,00%	8,33%
more than 9	7,69%	7,69%	30,77%	15,38%	38,46%	0,00%

Table 18.4.3 Rank your presence on Twitter as a marketing tool compared to Facebook, Google+, YouTube, LinkedIn. Broken out by Type of Organization

Type of Organization	No Answer	Ranked First	Ranked Second	Ranked Third	Ranked Fourth	Ranked Fifth
College	3,57%	3,57%	42,86%	21,43%	25,00%	3,57%
Other	30,00%	10,00%	50,00%	10,00%	0,00%	0,00%

Table 18.4.4 Rank your presence on Twitter as a marketing tool compared to Facebook, Google+, YouTube, LinkedIn. Broken out by Type of LinkedIn site

Type of LinkedIn site	No Answer	Ranked First	Ranked Second	Ranked Third	Ranked Fourth	Ranked Fifth
Uses Organizational LinkedIn Account	3,85%	7,69%	50,00%	15,38%	19,23%	3,85%
Uses Staff Member Personal LinkedIn Accounts	25,00%	0,00%	33,33%	25,00%	16,67%	0,00%

Table 18.4.5 Rank your presence on Twitter as a marketing tool compared to Facebook, Google+, YouTube, LinkedIn. Broken out by Type of LinkedIn Account

Type of LinkedIn Account	No Answer	Ranked First	Ranked Second	Ranked Third	Ranked Fourth	Ranked Fifth
Premium account	33,33%	0,00%	33,33%	16,67%	16,67%	0,00%
Basic account	6,25%	6,25%	46,88%	18,75%	18,75%	3,13%

Table 18.5.1 Rank your presence on YouTube as a marketing tool compared to Facebook, Google+, Twitter, LinkedIn

	No Answer	Ranked First	Ranked Second	Ranked Third	Ranked Fourth	Ranked Fifth
Entire sample	10,53%	0,00%	13,16%	39,47%	26,32%	10,53%

Table 18.5.2 Rank your presence on YouTube as a marketing tool compared to Facebook, Google+, Twitter, LinkedIn. Broken out by Number of FTE Fundraisers

Number of FTE Fundraisers	No Answer	Ranked First	Ranked Second	Ranked Third	Ranked Fourth	Ranked Fifth
less than 4	15,38%	0,00%	15,38%	38,46%	23,08%	7,69%
from 4 to 9	8,33%	0,00%	16,67%	50,00%	25,00%	0,00%
more than 9	7,69%	0,00%	7,69%	30,77%	30,77%	23,08%

Table 18.5.3 Rank your presence on YouTube as a marketing tool compared to Facebook, Google+, Twitter, LinkedIn. Broken out by Type of Organization

Type of Organization	No Answer	Ranked First	Ranked Second	Ranked Third	Ranked Fourth	Ranked Fifth
College	3,57%	0,00%	14,29%	39,29%	32,14%	10,71%
Other	30,00%	0,00%	10,00%	40,00%	10,00%	10,00%

Table 18.5.4 Rank your presence on YouTube as a marketing tool compared to Facebook, Google+, Twitter, LinkedIn. Broken out by Type of LinkedIn site

Type of LinkedIn site	No Answer	Ranked First	Ranked Second	Ranked Third	Ranked Fourth	Ranked Fifth
Uses Organizational LinkedIn Account	3,85%	0,00%	3,85%	42,31%	34,62%	15,38%
Uses Staff Member Personal LinkedIn Accounts	25,00%	0,00%	33,33%	33,33%	8,33%	0,00%

Table 18.5.5 Rank your presence on YouTube as a marketing tool compared to Facebook, Google+, Twitter, LinkedIn. Broken out by Type of LinkedIn Account

Type of LinkedIn Account	No Answer	Ranked First	Ranked Second	Ranked Third	Ranked Fourth	Ranked Fifth
Premium account	33,33%	0,00%	0,00%	0,00%	33,33%	33,33%
Basic account	6,25%	0,00%	15,63%	46,88%	25,00%	6,25%

SECTION H: JOB POSTS ON LINKEDIN

Table 19.1 Does your firm post available jobs on LinkedIn?

	No Answer	Yes	No
Entire sample	7,89%	23,68%	68,42%

Table 19.2 Does your firm post available jobs on LinkedIn? Broken out by Number of FTE Fundraisers

Number of FTE Fundraisers	No Answer	Yes	No
less than 4	0,00%	15,38%	84,62%
from 4 to 9	16,67%	33,33%	50,00%
more than 9	7,69%	23,08%	69,23%

Table 19.3 Does your firm post available jobs on LinkedIn? Broken out by Type of Organization

Type of Organization	No Answer	Yes	No
College	7,14%	17,86%	75,00%
Other	10,00%	40,00%	50,00%

Table 19.4 Does your firm post available jobs on LinkedIn? Broken out by Type of LinkedIn site

Type of LinkedIn site	No Answer	Yes	No
Uses Organizational LinkedIn Account	7,69%	30,77%	61,54%
Uses Staff Member Personal LinkedIn Accounts	8,33%	8,33%	83,33%

Table 19.5 Does your firm post available jobs on LinkedIn? Broken out by Type of LinkedIn Account

Type of LinkedIn Account	No Answer	Yes	No
Premium account	16,67%	16,67%	66,67%
Basic account	6,25%	25,00%	68,75%

Table 20.1 How much did your firm spend over the past year on job posts on LinkedIn? ($)

	Mean	Median	Minimum	Maximum
Entire sample	170,00	0,00	0,00	1000,00

Table 20.2 How much did your firm spend over the past year on job posts on LinkedIn? Broken out by Number of FTE Fundraisers

Number of FTE Fundraisers	Mean	Median	Minimum	Maximum
less than 4	0,00	0,00	0,00	0,00
from 4 to 9	290,00	80,00	0,00	1000,00
more than 9	175,00	0,00	0,00	1000,00

Table 20.3 How much did your firm spend over the past year on job posts on LinkedIn? Broken out by Type of Organization

Type of Organization	Mean	Median	Minimum	Maximum
College	100,00	0,00	0,00	1000,00
Other	403,33	160,00	50,00	1000,00

Table 20.4 How much did your firm spend over the past year on job posts on LinkedIn? Broken out by Type of LinkedIn site

Type of LinkedIn site	Mean	Median	Minimum	Maximum
Uses Organizational LinkedIn Account	186,36	0,00	0,00	1000,00
Uses Staff Member Personal LinkedIn Accounts	80,00	80,00	0,00	160,00

Table 20.5 How much did your firm spend over the past year on job posts on LinkedIn? Broken out by Type of LinkedIn Account

Type of LinkedIn Account	Mean	Median	Minimum	Maximum
Premium account	0,00	0,00	0,00	0,00
Basic account	184,17	0,00	0,00	1000,00

SECTION I: POLICIES ON LINKEDIN INVITATIONS AND USE OF INMAIL

What is the firm's policy on sending out LinkedIn Invitations?

1) Still in development
2) I don't know of the policy.
3) Unknown
4) do not know
5) N/A
6) We don't - we are a passive site
7) no known corporate policy
8) N/A
9) We don't send out invitations but respond to alumni and students and prospective students. At this time, we want to have a person's participation in LinkedIn serve as an indication of their independent interest and enthusiasm for the university and don't want to 'push' for involvement.
10) ?
11) Nothing written yet
12) No policy
13) We don't currently have a policy.
14) We have not done this.
15) None
16) we do not have a policy
17) None
18) N/A
19) We don't use LinkedIn
20) There is no policy but is in development
21) Have not used LinkedIn for invitations.
22) we don't have one
23) none
24) No policy.

Table 21.1 How many InMail messages does the firm send per month?

	Mean	Median	Minimum	Maximum
Entire sample	0,91	0,00	0,00	10,00

Table 21.2 How many InMail messages does the firm send per month? Broken out by Number of FTE Fundraisers

Number of FTE Fundraisers	Mean	Median	Minimum	Maximum
less than 4	2,00	0,00	0,00	10,00
from 4 to 9	0,00	0,00	0,00	0,00
more than 9	0,00	0,00	0,00	0,00

Table 21.3 How many InMail messages does the firm send per month? Broken out by Type of Organization

Type of Organization	Mean	Median	Minimum	Maximum
College	1,43	0,00	0,00	10,00
Other	0,00	0,00	0,00	0,00

Table 21.4 How many InMail messages does the firm send per month? Broken out by Type of LinkedIn site

Type of LinkedIn site	Mean	Median	Minimum	Maximum
Uses Organizational LinkedIn Account	1,43	0,00	0,00	10,00
Uses Staff Member Personal LinkedIn Accounts	0,00	0,00	0,00	0,00

Table 21.5 How many InMail messages does the firm send per month? Broken out by Type of LinkedIn Account

Type of LinkedIn Account	Mean	Median	Minimum	Maximum
Premium account	0,00	0,00	0,00	0,00
Basic account	1,00	0,00	0,00	10,00

Describe the process that your firm uses to develop LinkedIn profiles for your fundraisers. Do they write and post the profiles themselves? Are they edited by an online marketing specialist to insure proper key word usage and other practices to assure their effectiveness? What practices has your firm developed and what have been the results?

1) No policy exists.
2) This has not been done.
3) We don't control
4) write and post the profiles themselves
5) They write and post the profiles themselves.
6) There is no centrally managed process, all the staff do their own.
7) N/A
8) We have not been posting and, as yet, don't have a policy.
9) Self-posted
10) n/a
11) They do their own profiles
12) Fundraisers write their own profiles.
13) They are self-maintained. We have an occasional info session on best practices. Honesty and clarity are key. Transparency.
14) Self-generated
15) All self-initiated and completed
16) Each person is responsible for their own profile. They are not edited.
17) Individuals
18) Self-developed and edited.
19) It's all done on a completely personal, independent basis. It is not coordinated by the organization in any way.
20) N/A at this time
21) we haven't delved into fundraising in our groups or pages
22) None
23) They write the profiles themselves.

Does your organization have a policy of providing content, or content development assistance, to individuals so that they can promote the firm through their personal LinkedIn pages? If so what kind of assistance do you provide?

1) No.
2) do not know
3) No
4) People cannot fundraise for personal causes on our LinkedIn Page
5) No
6) N/A
7) We have not been providing content and, as yet, don't have a policy.
8) No
9) n/a
10) no policy
11) None
12) No.
13) No
14) No
15) No.
16) N/A
17) None
18) No.

Table 22.1 As an educated guess what percentage (%) of your LinkedIn updates from your organization's LinkedIn page include photos, videos or other visual materials?

	Mean	Median	Minimum	Maximum
Entire sample	14,29	0,00	0,00	80,00

Table 22.2 As an educated guess what percentage (%) of your LinkedIn updates from your organization's LinkedIn page include photos, videos or other visual materials? Broken out by Number of FTE Fundraisers

Number of FTE Fundraisers	Mean	Median	Minimum	Maximum
less than 4	0,00	0,00	0,00	0,00
from 4 to 9	3,75	2,50	0,00	10,00
more than 9	26,43	25,00	0,00	80,00

Table 22.3 As an educated guess what percentage (%) of your LinkedIn updates from your organization's LinkedIn page include photos, videos or other visual materials? Broken out by Type of Organization

Type of Organization	Mean	Median	Minimum	Maximum
College	20,00	7,50	0,00	80,00
Other	0,00	0,00	0,00	0,00

Table 22.4 As an educated guess what percentage (%) of your LinkedIn updates from your organization's LinkedIn page include photos, videos or other visual materials? Broken out by Type of LinkedIn site

Type of LinkedIn site	Mean	Median	Minimum	Maximum
Uses Organizational LinkedIn Account	15,38	0,00	0,00	80,00
Uses Staff Member Personal LinkedIn Accounts	0,00	0,00	0,00	0,00

Table 22.5 As an educated guess what percentage (%) of your LinkedIn updates from your organization's LinkedIn page include photos, videos or other visual materials? Broken out by Type of LinkedIn Account

Type of LinkedIn Account	Mean	Median	Minimum	Maximum
Premium account	37,50	37,50	25,00	50,00
Basic account	10,42	0,00	0,00	80,00

How would you advise your peers on the most effective ways to use LinkedIn?

1) Still investigating.
2) Watch John Hill's YouTube videos!
3) Start with having a page and keeping it up to date, follow and participate in groups that genuinely interest you
4) We have been advising peers and students to establish an account on Linked In.
5) Use it for young alumni, keeping databases current, and possible donor interests.
6) we only use it for research
7) not sure
8) University Pages are an extremely useful tool!
9) great research tool
10) Make sure you have a strong profile on LinkedIn - use the Advanced search - it will help you with just about any issue.
11) We don't have any advice yet since we are very new to using this resources.
12) I would be looking for this info myself.
13) No advice to give but welcome input from other colleges and universities
14) I would think I could learn from them better than we could learn from them
15) I would use it to gain contacts but not as a solicitation tool.

32108956R00047

Made in the USA
Charleston, SC
08 August 2014